Tweenies™

Counting up to 20

Written by Penny Coltman

'Come on, everyone,' called Bella.
'Let's play hide-and-seek!'

'I think it's your turn to
count, Jake,' said Fizz.

'Make sure you count up to twenty,' said Bella.

'Yeah – no cheating, mate,' chuckled Milo.

'I know I can count to ten,' said Jake. 'One, two, three, four . . . Oh dear, I'm not sure I can remember the rest.'

'I'll show you, Jakey,' said Milo. 'Look, we'll all help.'

one nose

and two ears

three bones

and four Tweenies

five boxes

and six circles

seven biscuits

and eight shoes

nine balloons

9

and ten fingers

10

'I've made a poster of all the numbers up to ten to help you remember them,' said Judy.

'One, two, three, four, five, six, seven, eight, nine, ten,' counted the Tweenies.

'But what comes next?' asked Jake.
'How do I count up to twenty?'

'I think we need a counting day,' answered Max.

'The number that comes
after ten is eleven,' said Bella.
'Look, here are eleven crayons.'

11

At messy time, the Tweenies made cakes with Judy.

'We have made twelve cakes,' said Judy.

'Can you count them, Jake?' asked Milo. 'How many can we have each?'

12

Everyone made collections of things for Jake to count.

Fizz found thirteen feathers.

Milo collected fourteen toy cars.

Judy brought in fifteen leaves.

Doodles made sixteen paw prints.

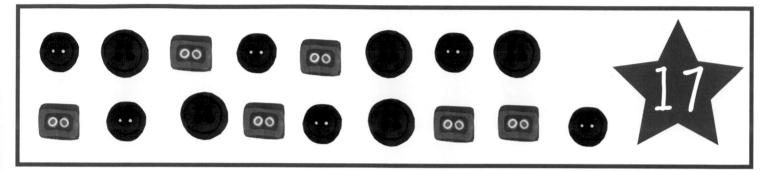

Max found seventeen buttons.

Bella and Milo collected eighteen flowers.

Judy found nineteen pencils that needed putting away!

'While you've all been busy collecting things to count, I've hidden twenty paintbrushes for you to find,' chuckled Max.

'Oh, let's find them all!' shouted the Tweenies, excitedly.

'I'm sure I've found the most,' boasted Bella.

'Well, I've got quite a lot too,' said Fizz.

'I found a brush,' said Jake, proudly.

'Well done, mate,' cried Milo.

'Have you found all the brushes?' asked Max.

'I've written down the numbers from ten to twenty to help you remember them,' laughed Judy. 'Will you paint them for me with your new paintbrushes?'

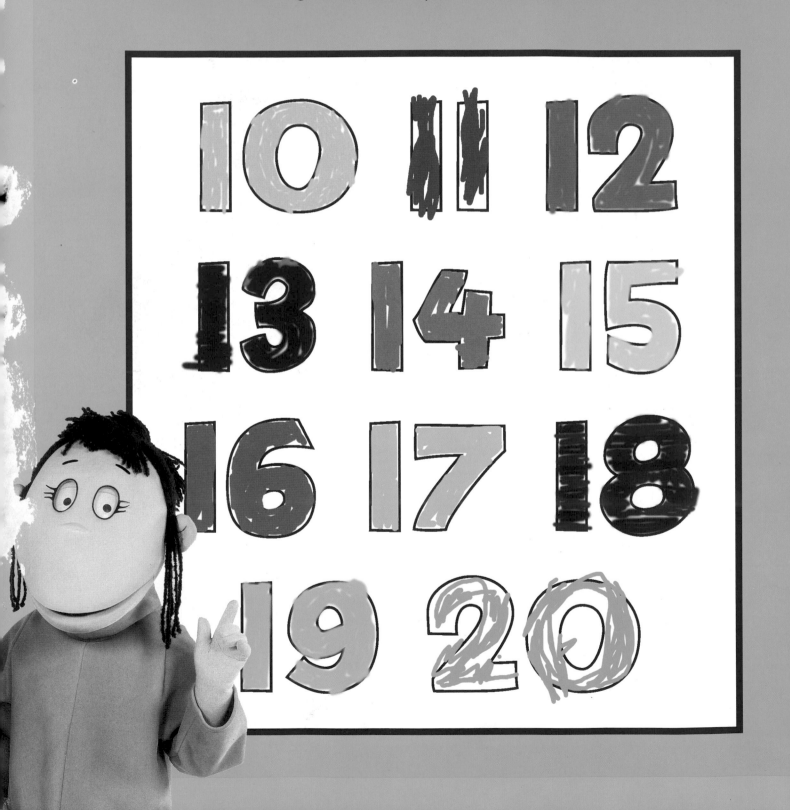

'I think I can count all the way to twenty now,'
said Jake. 'So, let's play hide-and-seek! Go and
hide, everybody!'

Now try our puzzle page!

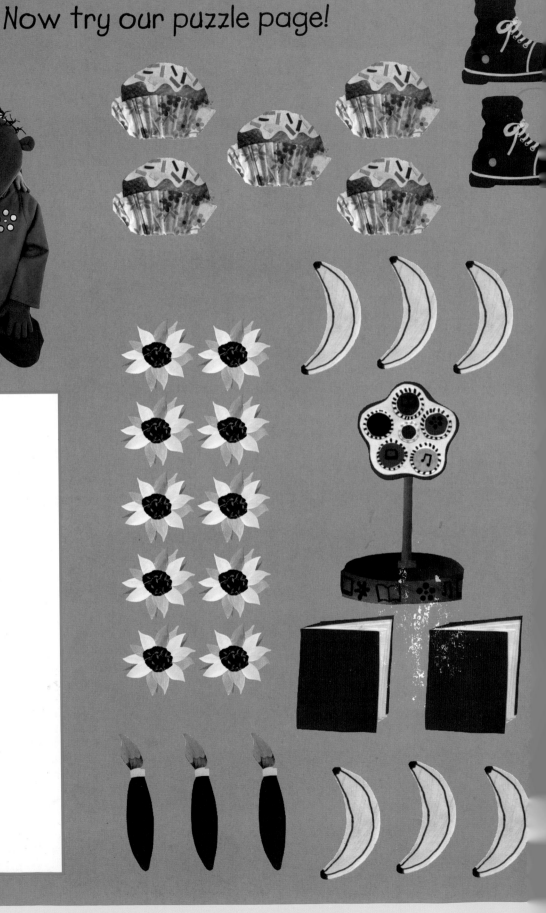

Find and count:

1 Tweenie clock

4 books

6 shoes

7 paintbrushes

10 cakes

12 bananas

15 butterflies

20 flowers

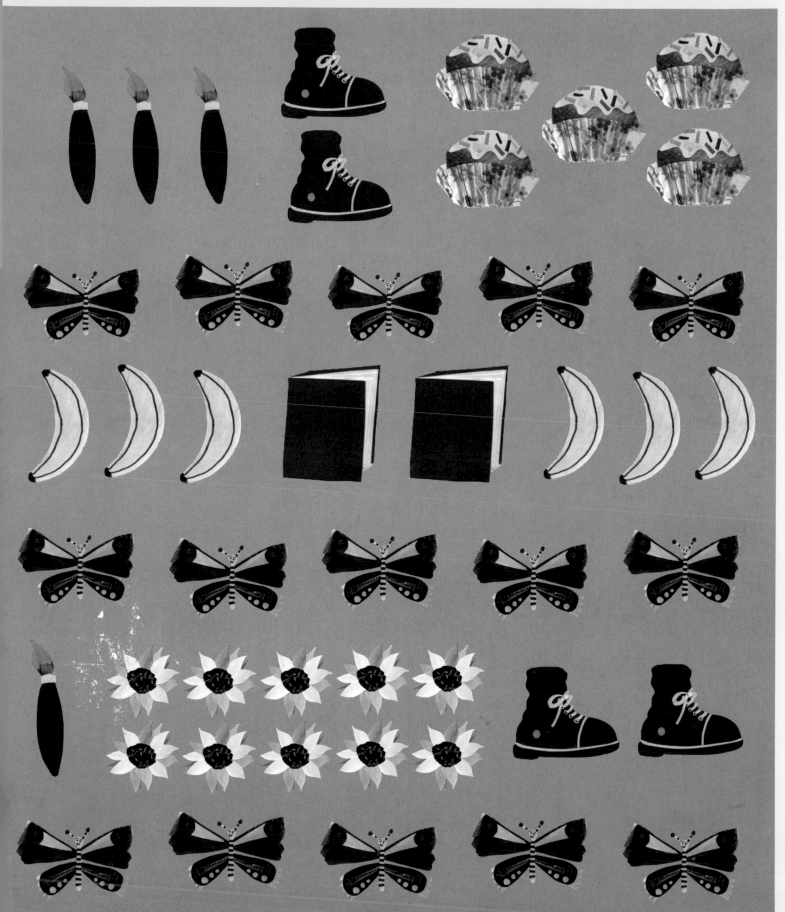

Goodbye

Parent's notes

Learning to count involves a number of skills, all of which you can help your child to develop through enjoying this book together. To be able to count, a child needs to:

- be able to say the numbers in the right order

- match one object or action to each number

- understand that the last number said when you count a set of things tells you how many things there are

- know that it doesn't matter in what order you count a set of things, the number of things in the set stays the same.

This book will help your child to understand how to count and why it is useful. The book also introduces number words and numerals up to 20. Although it is helpful for children starting school to recognise a few numbers, especially those up to 10, don't expect your child to know how all the numbers to 20 are written.

Pages 2-3

- Talk about the game of hide-and-seek, explaining that one person counts, by saying numbers in order, while the others hide.

Page 4

- Give your child plenty of practice in saying numbers in the correct order.

- Link each word to an action by counting stairs as you go up or down. Count the buttons as you fasten a coat, or count your steps as you walk along.

- Playing a number-track game in which you throw a dice and move a counter is a very good way of practising matching one move to one count.

Page 5

- Help your child to count the things in the pictures. Use the phrase 'How many?' to help your child to understand what counting is for. Encourage counting from left to right across the page, where possible. Show your child how to touch each object in turn as it is counted.

- Emphasise the last counting word in each case: 'Doodles has one, two, three bones. How many bones does he have?'

Page 6

- Talk about 'keeping count'. As you count the objects ask, 'Have we already counted that one?'

- Tip a small number of objects onto a table. Arrange them in a line and count from left to right, encouraging your child to touch or move each one as you count. Now spread the objects out and count them again. Does it make any difference to the number?

Page 7

- Help your child to see that starting to count in a different place makes no difference to the number of objects. Count the balloons from left to right and then from right to left. Does it make any difference?

- As your child becomes more confident, play tricks by counting one of the balloons twice or by missing out a number word. Does your child notice?

Page 8

- Point to each numeral in turn and say its name with your child. Play a 'Who can spot' game in which you challenge your child to find numbers as you say them.

- Try covering up one number. Can your child guess which number is hiding?

Page 9

- Encourage your child to become familiar with the order of the numbers up to ten as you sing songs together. Any counting songs are useful, but keep a special look out for those which count forwards rather than backwards.

Page 10

- Encourage your child to make collections of objects to count. Use toy cars to make traffic jams. Place a number of plastic animals on a paper 'field' and count them in and out through a pretend gate.

Page 11

- Use a large 'dozen' egg-box or a baking tray with a dozen wells as a counting tray. Show your child how to count up to twelve small objects by placing one on each well.

Pages 12-13

- Encourage your child to help you make collections of objects to count. Useful examples include spoons, toy bricks, buttons, leaves, shells or conkers.
- Play a counting 'grab' game in which you take turns to pick up a handful of the objects, tip them on to the table and count them.

Page 14

- Show your child how to count to twenty by counting all their fingers and toes. As confidence grows, try counting backwards!

Page 15

- Encourage your child to find all the paintbrushes that Max has hidden. The main challenge of this page is to accurately keep count, remembering which brushes have been counted.
- Support this by placing a piece of greaseproof paper over the page and marking off each brush as it is counted.

Pages 16-17

- These pages are about comparing numbers. Introduce ideas of 'more' and 'most'. Who has found the most brushes? Has Fizz found more than Milo or not as many?

Pages 18-19

- Point to each number in turn and say its name. Talk about <u>before</u> and <u>after</u>, encouraging your child to become familiar with the order of the numbers to 20. For example, 'Look, number 12 comes after number 11' or 'Here's number 19 and the next number is 20.'

Pages 20-21

- Take turns in completing counting challenges as you and your child choose objects for each other to find and count.

Stickers and inside cover

- Show your child how to choose a sticker and to count the objects illustrated on it.
- Then help him or her find that number on the inside cover.
- Now encourage your child to place the sticker over the number.